SPORTS
STARTERS

Stretch it
Yoga

Kyla Wilson

Crabtree Publishing Company

www.crabtreebooks.com

SPORTS STARTERS

Created by Bobbie Kalman

Author
Kyla Wilson

Project coordinator
Kathy Middleton

Editors
Molly Aloian
Kathryn White

Proofreader
Wendy Scavuzzo

Photo research
Melissa McClellan

Design
Tibor Choleva
Melissa McClellan

Production coordinator
Margaret Amy Salter

Prepress technician
Margaret Amy Salter

Print coordinator
Katherine Berti

Consultant
Sandee Ewasiuk, Down Dog Yoga, certified yoga instructor

Special thanks to
Kaya Shimizu, Luke Siefker, Morgyn Roberts, Jacob Cheng, Daniel Lesiuk, Angela Shimizu, David Church, and Zach Murphy

Illustrations
Leif Peng: page 9

Photographs
© Lincoln Adler (p 26)
© Marc Crabtree (front cover)
Dreamstime.com: © Ron Chapple (back cover, pp 10, 15, 16, 30)
Getty Images: © Narinder Nanu (p 27)
iStockphoto.com: © Joseph C. Justice Jr. (titlepage); © Vladimir Surkov (p 5)
© Lindsey Ryder: pp 6, 7, 11, 12, 13, 14, 17, 18, 19, 20, 21, 22, 23, 25, 31
Shutterstock.com: © Artur Bogacki (p 24); © Mayskyphoto (p 29)
© Robert Sturman (p 28)
Thinkstock: © iStockphoto (toc page); © Creatas (p 4)

Created for Crabtree Publishing by BlueApple*Works*

Library and Archives Canada Cataloguing in Publication

Wilson, Kyla
  Stretch it yoga / Kyla Wilson.

(Sports starters)
Includes index.
Issued also in electronic format.
ISBN 978-0-7787-3153-5 (bound).--ISBN 978-0-7787-3164-1 (pbk.)

  1. Hatha yoga--Juvenile literature. I. Title.
II. Series: Sports starters (St. Catharines, Ont.)

RA781.7.W567 2012   j613.7'046   C2012-900885-0

Library of Congress Cataloging-in-Publication Data

CIP available at Library of Congress

Crabtree Publishing Company

Printed in the U.S.A./032012/CJ20120215

www.crabtreebooks.com   1-800-387-7650

Published in Canada
Crabtree Publishing
616 Welland Ave.
St. Catharines, Ontario
L2M 5V6

Published in the United States
Crabtree Publishing
PMB 59051
350 Fifth Avenue, 59th Floor
New York, New York 10118

Published in the United Kingdom
Crabtree Publishing
Maritime House
Basin Road North, Hove
BN41 1WR

Published in Australia
Crabtree Publishing
3 Charles Street
Coburg North
VIC 3058

Contents

What is yoga?

Yoga is a type of exercise that strengthens your body and your mind. People have been doing yoga for more than 5,000 years. The word yoga means "joined" in **Sanskrit**. Yoga joins your body and your mind. People who practice yoga are called **yogis**. There are many types of yoga. The most popular type is called **Hatha yoga**.

You need good balance to try some yoga poses.

Yoga can make you feel calm and strong.

Just relax!

One of the best things about yoga is that it helps people relax. For example, it can help kids relax before they take a test. It also makes the body stronger and more **flexible**. It improves balance and **posture**, too. Yoga also helps many people to think clearly and **concentrate**.

Getting ready

Yoga does not require a lot of equipment. All you need is a yoga mat to stand and lie on. A thin sticky mat helps to stop your feet slipping when you stretch. Yogis wear loose and comfortable clothes when practicing yoga. They can wear socks or go barefoot.

*Yoga improves muscle tone, flexibility, strength, and **stamina**.*

Using blocks for standing poses is very helpful, especially if one hand is reaching to the floor.

Yoga Props

A yoga teacher can explain how to use **blocks** and **straps**. Yoga blocks and straps can provide extra support. Yoga teachers help students use these pieces of equipment in the most effective ways.

In the yoga studio

Yoga studios are fun places! They are large enough that students can stretch out on mats without touching each other. Students are careful not to step on anyone's mat when they move around the room. The yoga studio is a quiet place, and is not too cool or too hot. Many yogis prefer to practice yoga on an empty stomach because it is easier to breathe, bend, and stretch. Many yogis drink a lot of water after doing yoga.

Every yoga class begins and ends with the teacher and students saying "**Namaste**." This means "I bow to you" in Sanskrit. As they say this, students bow their heads, put their palms together in front of their chests, and close their eyes. Doing this helps to calm their minds and relax their bodies.

yoga mat

a typical yoga studio

Breathe in

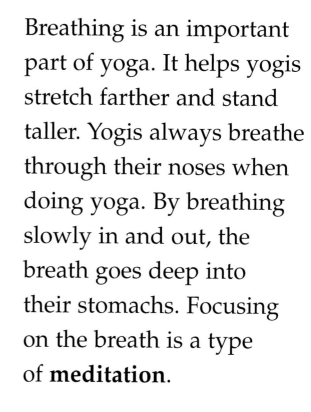

Breathing is an important part of yoga. It helps yogis stretch farther and stand taller. Yogis always breathe through their noses when doing yoga. By breathing slowly in and out, the breath goes deep into their stomachs. Focusing on the breath is a type of **meditation**.

This kind of deep breathing calms the yogis. When they are calm, their minds relax. This helps them to think better.

*Yogis can feel their stomachs move up and down when they **inhale** and **exhale**.*

Mudras can be used with almost any yoga pose.

Hold your hand

Some yogis use hand gestures to help them focus on their yoga poses and their breathing. Each hand gesture is called a **mudra**. In some mudras, one finger touches the thumb of the same hand.

Warming up

During yoga, people do poses called **asanas**. Before beginning the asanas, yogis warm up their bodies by breathing deeply and stretching lightly. This gives them energy and prepares their bodies to move and to hold asanas for several seconds or minutes.

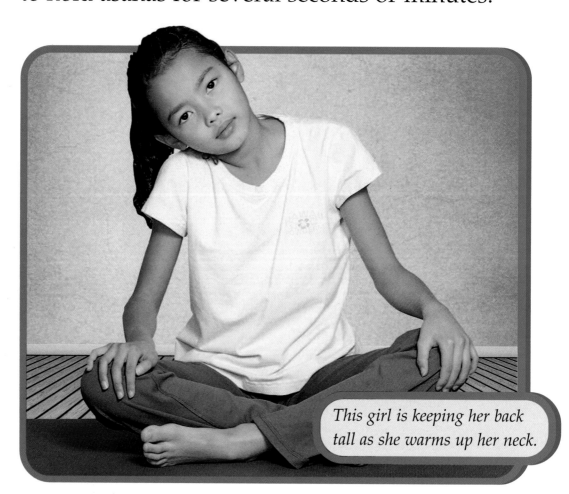

This girl is keeping her back tall as she warms up her neck.

Getting warmer

As yogis relax and warm up their bodies, they keep breathing deeply, in and out. This helps them to stretch their bodies farther. Breathing deeply warms up their minds for yoga, too! It clears their heads and prepares them to focus on the asanas.

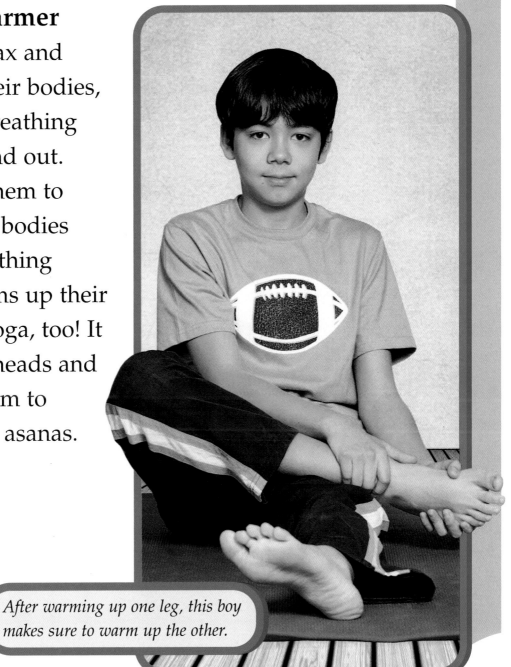

After warming up one leg, this boy makes sure to warm up the other.

Standing tall

Yoga improves your posture. Good posture can help you feel secure and brave. It is hard to think of anything more solid than a mountain. For Mountain Pose, yogis stand straight with their feet slightly apart. They feel the ground solid under their feet. They breathe in and out, and they concentrate on feeling strong and relaxed.

Keep your chest open in Mountain Pose.

Solid as a tree

Tree Pose makes yogis feel tall and strong. Yogis feel their breath running throughout their bodies—the way sap flows through a tree. The arms and legs are strong like the roots and branches of a tree. Yogis spread their arms like a tree with a lot of branches.

In Tree Pose, you stand on one leg first, then the other.

Stretch!

During asanas, yogis stretch then relax. Some asanas are performed standing up. Others are done sitting or kneeling. Some asanas are done lying on the stomach or the back. Warrior Pose stretches the body. It also makes the body feel strong, from the feet all the way to the fingertips.

A yoga teacher is helping this student get into position.

Child's Pose will make you feel calm and relaxed.

After stretching

Yoga should never hurt. A yogi knows that if a pose is painful, he or she can move into a different pose that feels better. Child's Pose is an easy, relaxing asana. In this pose, a yogi breathes deeply. The back and shoulders relax. The yogi holds the pose for a few minutes, and raises the head slowly to sit up.

Cats and dogs

Many yoga poses are named after animals. For example, Cat Pose, Cobra Pose, and Lion Pose are named after animals. Cat Pose is great for stretching your back. To do this pose, you breathe in as you lift your head so your back curves. Then you breathe out and arch your back— just like a cat!

Cat Pose stretches your back and shoulders.

In Downward Dog, you spread your fingers like big wide paws.

Downward Dog

Have you ever watched a puppy stretch after a nap? Downward Dog is a pose that will stretch your back, shoulders, and legs. Your head hangs down, which sends more blood and **oxygen** to your head. Many yogis think more clearly after doing Downward Dog.

Yoga with a friend

It is fun doing yoga with a friend. You can work together to improve your poses. Maybe you know an asana your friend does not. You can share it! Practicing yoga with a friend will help you focus. You can also work together on poses that need good balance.

Boat Pose strengthens your stomach, back, and shoulders.

You and a friend can stretch your hips and backs with See-saw Pose.

Laugh a lot

When you practice yoga asanas with a friend, you may find yourself laughing. Laughing is good for you because it makes you breathe deeply. When you breathe deeply, you take in a lot of air, which is good for your mind and body. Laugh and have fun when you try yoga with a friend!

Noisy yoga

Some asanas involve making noise. In Cobra Pose, yogis imagine their bodies slowly slithering like a snake's body. Some yogis even hiss like a snake. They must still remember to breathe deeply. A pose that bends the body backward, such as Cobra Pose, is always followed by a pose that bends the body forward. The body is bent forward during Child's Pose.

Cobra Pose can make your back stronger.

Stick out your tongue and stretch your fingers wide when you roar in Lion Pose!

Roar!

Lion Pose is a great way to stretch your arms and upper legs. The muscles in your face also get a workout. You should feel a stretch from the tip of your tongue up to your forehead. Lion Pose also makes you feel brave. Some yogis roar as they tilt their heads back.

Twist it

In some yoga poses, you twist your body. Twisting increases flexibility and strengthens the **spine** and stomach. Some yogis stand and twist. Others sit on a mat to twist. They keep their shoulders down and focus on slowly twisting the spine.

*Twisted Chair Pose wakes up your belly and helps with **digestion**.*

Try Seated Spinal Twist on both sides of your body.

Breathe and twist

Be sure to move slowly and smoothly as you twist. Remember to breathe deeply. You may find that the deeper you breathe, the more you can twist. It is important to work each side of your body, because balance is one of the goals of yoga. So when yogis twist one way, they always twist the other way, too.

Hold that pose

At a yoga competition, you can learn a lot. Watch other yogis to see how you can improve your own poses. All the competitors have the same amount of time to perform their poses. In a yoga competition, each competitor performs a series of seven postures in three minutes. The first five poses are required and the last two are the competitor's choice.

This girl is competing in a yoga competition.

Judges may walk around each competitor to observe their performance.

Judging

Judges give points to decide who wins the contest. They watch how each yogi moves from pose to pose. The judges check that everyone is performing each asana correctly. Yogis get points for balance and how well they bend. Judges may walk around each competitor to observe the asana from all sides.

Yoga stars

Some of the yogis you see at competitions are amazing! Famous yogis practice yoga several times a day. They can balance and bend their bodies easily. They are good at breathing smoothly, too. You can learn a lot from watching these yogis.

Brandy Lyn Winfield is one of the top yogis in the world.

Other famous yogis

Many top athletes take yoga classes. Yoga makes them stronger and improves their balance. Yoga also helps athletes focus on their breathing. Basketball star Shaquille O'Neal is a yogi. Tennis superstars Venus Williams and Serena Williams take yoga classes, too.

Shaquille O'Neal is so tall he needed two mats to span his extra-long limbs.

Namaste

Before finishing a yoga class, the teacher makes sure that all the students are relaxed. The students enjoy taking slow, deep breaths. While they inhale and exhale, they concentrate on their stomachs moving in and out. They focus on each part of their bodies and notice even the smallest sensations, such as how their legs feel touching the mat.

Feel your breath go slowly in and out.

At the end of a yoga session, relax your body and mind.

Relax your mind

At the end of their practice, yogis always do the Corpse Pose. It is a resting pose. They focus on their body and breathing. Maybe they use a mudra to quiet and still their minds. At the end of the class, the teacher and students say "Namaste" to each other and bow.

Namaste!

Glossary

Note: Boldfaced words that are defined in the text may not appear in the glossary.

asanas Yoga poses

blocks Objects, usually made of foam or wood, used in yoga to help achieve proper pose and maintain stability

concentrate To focus one's attention on one thing

digestion The process of absorbing nutrients from food

exhale Breathe out

flexible Able to bend easily

Hatha yoga Slow, gentle yoga

inhale Breathe in

meditation Spending time in quiet thought

mudra Hand gesture or pose

Namaste A yoga greeting. It means "I bow to you."

oxygen A colorless, odorless, and tasteless gas that makes up about 20 percent of the air we breathe

posture General way of holding the body

Sanskrit An ancient Indic language of India

spine The bones of the back

stamina Ability to sustain prolonged physical or mental effort

straps Long cotton belts used in yoga that allow you to grasp your limbs that you could not reach otherwise

yogis People who teach or practice yoga

Index